BECOMING A WOMAN OF PRAYER

A BIBLE STUDY BY CYNTHIA HEALD

NAVPRESS

BRINGING TRUTH TO LIFE

NavPress Publishing Group

P.O. Box 35001, Colorado Springs, Colorado 80935

© 1996 by Cynthia Heald
All rights reserved. No part of this publication may be reproduced in any form without written permission from NavPress, P.O. Box 35001, Colorado Springs, CO 80935.
ISBN 08910-99549

Cover illustration: Jess Nishinaka/Bernstein & Andriulli Inc.

Unless otherwise identified, all Scripture quotations in this publication are taken from the *New American Standard Bible* (NASB), © The Lockman Foundation 1960, 1962, 1963, 1968, 1971, 1972, 1973, 1975, 1977; the *HOLY BIBLE: NEW INTERNATIONAL VERSION®* (NIV®), Copyright © 1973, 1978, 1984 by International Bible Society, used by permission of Zondervan Publishing House, all rights reserved; *The Message* (MSG) by Eugene H. Peterson, copyright © 1993, 1994, 1995, 1996, used by permission of NavPress Publishing Group; *The Living Bible* (TLB), © 1971 owned by assignment by the Illinois Regional Bank N.A. (as trustee), used by permission of Tyndale House Publishers, Inc., Wheaton, IL 60189; and the *Amplified New Testament* (AMP), © The Lockman Foundation 1954, 1958.

Printed in the United States of America

3 4 5 6 7 8 9 10 11 12 13 14 15 / 99 98 97

CONTENTS

SUGGESTIONS FOR HOW TO USE THIS STUDY

This study is designed for both individual as well as small group use, and for women of any age or family status.

Many of the questions will guide you into Scripture passages. Ask God to reveal His truth to you through His Word, and don't be concerned about "wrong" answers. Bible study references—such as commentaries, encyclopedias, and handbooks—can help you understand particular passages by providing historical background, contexts, and common interpretations. (In a few cases, you'll need access to a standard dictionary—such as Webster's, Random House, or the Oxford American—for general word definitions.) Other questions will ask you to reflect on your own life. Approach these questions honestly and thoughtfully; however, if you're doing this study in a group, don't feel that you must reveal private details of your life experiences.

This study will encourage you to grow in your intimacy with God by exploring what the Bible teaches about prayer. But studying about prayer should never be a substitute for prayer itself. Therefore, each session begins and ends with prayer. To open your study, a prayer of preparation has been selected from the voices of Christian saints. In closing, you will be invited to write a brief prayer as a way of verbalizing to the Lord the insights and responses He has prompted. Your reflections will be enriched as you immerse them in prayer. However, the Bible reveals that prayer and the Scriptures are intertwined—and so you may want to begin memorizing the suggested Scripture passage at the start of each session. Let it dwell richly within you as you study and pray. The last chapter in *Becoming a Woman of Prayer* is a guide to spending time alone with God—for a brief interlude or a day-long retreat. If you are meeting in a group for this last session, separate for personal time with the Lord and then gather to share your experiences or to close in collective prayer.

The quotations from classic thinkers and writers have been carefully selected to enhance your understanding and enjoyment of the content in *Becoming a Woman of Prayer*. The references for these quotations (see the *Notes* section at the back of the book) furnish an excellent devotional reading list.

PREFACE

"It's me, it's me, it's me, O Lord, standing in the need of prayer" is a song I learned as a little girl. The words are still true for me as an older woman. Not only do I need prayer as others intercede for me, but I *stand in the need* of spending time in prayer.

I wrote this study because of my need for prayer. God made it very clear to me that it was about time I began to deepen my prayer life and the best way to get started was with *Becoming a Woman of Prayer*. This is a wonderful aspect of God's character: He shows us our need and then He creatively begins to meet that need.

If you desire to deepen your understanding of prayer so that you can pray more effectively and draw closer to our Lord, then perhaps this guide is for you too.

During my study of this subject I have prayed, wept, and been deeply challenged. The prayers of the saints in the Scriptures have helped me verbalize my prayers, and the prayers of godly saints have touched my heart. The passages on prayer have informed me and taught me how to pray biblically. The underlying principle of prayer, which overwhelmed me, is that God desires to be intimate with me, and He wants this relationship so much that He invites, encourages, and helps me to pray.

With such an incredible invitation from our Father extended to me, I realized that I would be unwise to refuse such an offer of fellowship and participation in His plans. So I have just begun to enter into the inner room and pray. I invite you to join me, but more importantly God invites you to join Him.

God bless you richly as you study. I pray that your life will never be the same because of your desire to become a woman of prayer.

—CYNTHIA HEALD

7

The chief object of prayer is to glorify the Lord Jesus.
We are to ask in Christ's name
"that the Father may be glorified in the Son" (John xiv. 13).
Listen! We are not to seek wealth or health, prosperity or success,
ease or comfort, spirituality or fruitfulness in service
simply for our own enjoyment or advancement or popularity,
but only for Christ's sake—for His glory.

—From *The Kneeling Christian*

CHAPTER ONE

AN INVITATION TO INTIMACY

*"Call to me and I will answer you
and tell you great and unsearchable things
you do not know."*
JEREMIAH 33:3, NIV

*What if God does not demand prayer
as much as gives prayer? What if God
wants prayer in order to satisfy us?
What if prayer is a means of God
nourishing, restoring, healing, converting us?
Suppose prayer is primarily allowing ourselves
to be loved, addressed and claimed by God.
What if praying means opening ourselves
to the gift of God's own self and presence?
What if our part in prayer is primarily
letting God be giver? Suppose prayer is not
a duty but the opportunity to experience
healing and transforming love?*[1]
MARTIN SMITH

The eternal, sovereign, majestic God of the universe wants to be intimate with us! He wants us to call, to cry, to sing to Him. He longs to love, to refresh, to encourage us. He wants to answer our call and to tell us great and unsearchable thoughts. God wants us to know that He is always ready to commune; He is always ready to listen. He wants to be so much a part of our lives that we would naturally come to Him at all times. He tells us that we have freedom to call to Him wherever we are, about anything on our hearts. He delights in being involved with His children, and prayer is His gift and His invitation to intimacy.

Prayer of Preparation

As you begin this chapter, pray with Julian of Norwich (fourteenth century) for a desire to respond to God's call to intimacy: *what precisely is he asking you?*

> God, of your goodness, give me yourself; for you are sufficient for me. I cannot properly ask anything less, to be worthy of you. If I were to ask less, I should always be in want. In you alone do I have all.[2]

God Invites Us to Pray

1. God continually declares His desire for fellowship with us. How do the following Scriptures portray God's desire for our intimacy with Him?

Jeremiah 29:11-14 *For I know the plans I have for you says the Lord, plans to prosper you and not harm you, plans to give you a hope and a future. then you will call on me, come & pray to me and I will listen to you. you will seek me and find me when you seek me with all your heart. I will be found by you declares the Lord and I will bring you back from captivity.*

Romans 8:14-17 *those who are led by God's Spirit are sons of god. For you did not receive a spirit that makes you a slave to fear but you received the Spirit of Sonship. ... We are God's children - heirs of God & co-heirs with Christ - if we share in his sufferings we may share in His Glory.*

Revelation 3:14-22 *you're lukewarm, you say you have everything but you're naked Buy gold, white clothes & eye salve from me those whom I love I rebuke & discipline I stand at the door and knock. If anyone opens the door I come in and eat with him. To him who over comes I give the right to sit with me on my throne*

12

> To pray is to let Jesus come into our hearts. This teaches us, in the first place, that it is not our prayer which moves the Lord Jesus. It is Jesus who moves us to pray. He knocks. Thereby He makes known His desire to come in to us. Our prayers are always a result of Jesus' knocking at our hearts' doors.[3]
> O. HALLESBY

2. Because God has reconciled us to Himself through the redemption offered through Jesus Christ, we can respond to God's invitation. What assurance of our access to our heavenly Father is offered in Hebrews 4:14-16? *Jesus is our High Priest. We can approach the throne of grace with confidence, so that we may receive mercy and find grace to help us in our time of need.*

> It is a throne set up on purpose for the dispensation of grace and from which every utterance is an utterance of grace. The scepter that is stretched out from it is the silver scepter of grace. The decrees proclaimed from it are purposes of grace. The gifts that are scattered down its golden steps are gifts of grace, and He who sits upon the throne is grace Himself. That it is the throne of grace that we approach when we pray is a mighty source of encouragement to all of us who are praying men and women.[4]
> CHARLES SPURGEON

3. Think back on your experience with God. What has been your idea of prayer: our going to God or God coming to us? Why? *My going to God. Did not know otherwise, even tho I know these scriptures. In '94, I prayed "Help me, Lord." He answered by giving me love, love + more love for all concerned. PTL*

4. Often my prayer is for God to show me how to please Him. I think in terms of active *doing* with people, but God receives pleasure from our wanting to *be* with Him! What do these verses indicate about how God receives our prayers?

Psalm 141:1-2 *may my prayer be set before you like incense; may the lifting up of my hands be like the evening sacrifice*

Like a sacrifice

Revelation 8:3-4 *incense + prayers went up in smoke before God — a pleasing sacrifice*

There is a fourfold resemblance between them [prayer and incense]: 1. In that it was beaten and pounded before it was used. So doth acceptable prayer proceed from a broken and contrite heart. 2. It was of no use until fire was put under it, and that taken from the altar. Nor is that prayer of any virtue or efficacy which is not kindled by the fire from above, the Holy Spirit of God, which we have from our altar, Christ Jesus. 3. It naturally ascended upwards towards heaven, as all offerings in the Hebrew are called "ascensions," risings up. 4. It yielded a sweet savour; which was one end of it in temple services, wherein there was so much burning of flesh and blood. So doth prayer yield a sweet savour unto God; a savour of rest, wherein he is well pleased.[5]

JOHN OWEN

5. Reflect for a moment on the promise of God's joy in experiencing intimacy with you. How does this influence your attitude toward prayer? *Changes my prayers as something I should do to something I delight in because it pleases my Lord*

AUTHOR'S REFLECTION

Realizing that God is committed to answering when I call with great and unsearchable revelations fills me with awe and humility. Understanding that God wants to impart spiritual strength and refreshment encourages me to feel that I don't have to come with a full agenda when I meet with God. *He* has invited *me*—and so I respond by choosing to answer His request for fellowship. How good it is to view prayer as an opportunity to receive from the Lord and as a time to "yield a sweet savour unto God."

Desiring intimacy with God ought to be the delight of my life and a choice gladly made. I think of Daniel. It didn't matter what the decrees were or what his schedule was; nothing kept him from his time with God. Certainly God revealed to Daniel incredible things he did not know. I am deeply aware of my need for this remarkable reminder from the Lord about how much He desires to bless me.

He invites us, and He waits for us to call.

> When a man is born from above, the life of the Son of God is born in him, and he can either starve that life or nourish it. Prayer is the way the life of God is nourished. Our ordinary views of prayer are not found in the New Testament. We look upon prayer as a means of getting things for ourselves; the Bible's idea of prayer is that we may get to know God Himself.[6]
> OSWALD CHAMBERS

A Prayer for Intimacy

David's heartfelt desire was to respond to God's call to intimacy.
In response to your study in this chapter, pray the following
prayer of David. Consider adding your own prayer to be sensitive to how God is calling you to deeper intimacy with Him.

DAVID'S PRAYER

Hear, O Lord, when I cry with my voice,
And be gracious to me and answer me.
When Thou didst say, "Seek My face," my heart
    said to Thee,
"Thy face, O Lord, I shall seek." (Psalm 27:7-8)

MY PRAYER

Lord, thank you that you hear when I call. Thank you that you desire to be intimate with me. Lord show me how to please you.

Suggested Scripture Memory

Jeremiah 33:3

CHAPTER TWO

PRAYING IN FAITH

*But let him ask in faith without any doubting,
for the one who doubts is like the surf of the sea
driven and tossed by the wind. For let not that
man expect that he will receive anything
from the Lord, being a double-minded man,
unstable in all his ways.*
JAMES 1:6-7

*We need not exert ourselves
and try to force ourselves to believe,
or try to chase doubt out of our hearts.
Both are just as useless.
It begins to dawn on us that
we can bring everything to Jesus,
no matter how difficult it is;
and we need not be frightened away
by our doubts or our weak faith,
but only tell Jesus how weak our faith is.
We have let Jesus into our hearts.
And He will fulfill our hearts' desires.*[1]
O. HALLESBY

Knowing that God wants our communion encourages us to pray. But there is a necessary element to prayer that God needs from us in order for our prayers to be answered. What God wants is our faith. Faith is belief, trust, dependence, and confidence. John D. Grassmic writes, "Faith that rests in God is unwavering trust in His omnipotent power and unfailing goodness."[2] If we go to a certain friend with a special request, we usually go and ask because we believe that friend can and will help us. So it is with the Lord. It pleases Him when we ask believing that He hears and will answer.

Prayer of Preparation

As you begin to study, pray with Thomas à Kempis (fourteenth and fifteenth centuries) for increased faith.

> Give us, O Lord, steadfast hearts that cannot be dragged down by false loves; give us courageous hearts that cannot be worn down by trouble; give us righteous hearts that cannot be sidetracked by unholy or unworthy goals. Give to us also, our Lord and God, understanding to know you, diligence to look for you, wisdom to recognize you, and a faithfulness that will bring us to see you face to face.[3]

Faith in God

1. Paul writes in Ephesians that we have boldness and confident access to God through faith in Jesus Christ (Ephesians 3:12). In the Upper Room Jesus teaches the importance of faith and its relationship to prayer. Read John 14:8-15, and write down all you learn about prayer from these verses.

2. Jesus clearly taught the disciples the value of faith. Read
   Mark 11:20-26 and indicate Jesus' instructions concerning
   prayer.

19

3. Unwavering faith in God's ways of answering prayer is essential. What do these Scriptures teach us about how to pray, based on our confidence before God?

James 1:5-8

1 John 5:13-15

> Believing what God says in His Word is faith.
> If I am to have faith when I pray, I must find some
> promise in the Word of God on which to rest my faith.
> Faith furthermore comes through the Spirit. The Spirit
> knows the will of God, and if I pray in the Spirit, and
> look to the Spirit to teach me God's will, He will lead me
> out in prayer along the line of that will, and give me faith
> that the prayer is to be answered; but in no case does
> real faith come by simply determining that you are
> going to get the thing that you want to get.
> If there is no promise in the Word of God, and no clear
> leading of the Spirit, there can be no real faith,
> and there should be no upbraiding of self
> for lack of faith in such a case.[6]
> R. A. TORREY

4. Faith is certainly a critical element of prayer. In light of the verses you have just studied, how would you characterize your faith when you pray?

AUTHOR'S REFLECTION

I have four lovely grown children. Suppose one of them called me and said, "Mom, I'd like to ask you to come stay with our children, but there will be a friend of ours here to be with you because I'm afraid you might take something or that you might mistreat one of the children." What would I think? Would I go? How would I respond?

In a way, this is what God is trying to communicate when He says that we must have faith when we call upon Him. I love my children very deeply and when they call and ask me for help or counsel in any way, they know that I will respond. They have faith in me because of our love relationship.

Also, because my children know me well, they would never ask me to do something that would compromise my character, and they would trust my discernment for what I thought would be the best way to answer their request.

And so it is with God: It pleases Him when we turn to Him in dependence and trust. When we ask in His Son's name, according to His character, God delights in proving His love, His wisdom, and His trustworthiness. As we experience His faithfulness we can sing, "My faith looks up to Thee, Thou Lamb of Calvary, Savior divine!"[7] Our faith is never misplaced when it is placed in Him.

> Mind you, He does not say to all men, "I will give you
> whatever you ask." That would be an unkind kindness.
> But He speaks to His disciples who have already received
> great grace at His hands. It is to disciples He commits
> this marvelous power of prayer.[8]
> CHARLES SPURGEON

A Prayer for Faith
David expresses his faith in God in Psalm 18. Pray along with
his thoughts and add your own prayer for your trust in God's
goodness and sufficiency.

DAVID'S PRAYER

"I love thee, O LORD, my strength."
The LORD is my rock and my fortress and my deliverer,
My God, my rock, in whom I take refuge;
My shield and the horn of my salvation, my stronghold.
I call upon the LORD, who is worthy to be praised,
And I am saved from my enemies.
(Psalm 18:1-3)

MY PRAYER

Suggested Scripture Memory
James 1:5-7

22

CHAPTER THREE

GOD'S HELP IN PRAYER

*And in the same way
the Spirit also helps our weakness;
for we do not know how to pray as we should,
but the Spirit Himself intercedes for us
with groanings too deep for words.*
ROMANS 8:26

*Prayer is not getting the Lord's attention,
but allowing Him to lead us in praying
for what He is more ready to give
than we may be to ask.*[1]
LLOYD JOHN OGILVIE

God wants us to know Him, fellowship with Him, and trust Him. But He doesn't leave it up to us to find out how to reach Him through prayer; He provides His blessed Holy Spirit to help us. For those of us who often feel that we just don't know how to pray, this is very good news! God's Spirit intercedes for us when we come to Him. This is another confirmation of how much God wants us to pray. He asks only that we bring to Him a deep longing to abide in Him by faith. How blessed we are to be in relationship with our God, who gives us all we need for a life of prayer.

Prayer of Preparation
As you begin this session, pray with S. D. Gordon (twentieth century) that you might rely on God more deeply for His support in your life of prayer:

> Holy Spirit, be praying in me the thing the Father wants done. Father, what the Spirit within me is praying, that is my prayer in Jesus' name. Thy will, what Thou art wishing and thinking, may that be fully done here.[2]

God's Spirit

1. God knows our weakness in prayer, and He wants to help us. How do the following Scriptures describe His support?

   Romans 8:26-34

   Hebrews 7:23-25

24

> The Holy Spirit helps us in our weaknesses, gives wisdom to our ignorance, turns ignorance into wisdom, and changes our weakness into strength. The Spirit himself does this. He helps and takes hold with us as we tug and toil. . . . He pleads for us and in us. He quickens, illumines, and inspires our prayers. He proclaims and elevates the matter of our prayers, and inspires the words and feelings of our prayers. He works mightily in us so that we can pray mightily. He enables us to pray always and ever according to the will of God.[3]
>
> E. M. BOUNDS

2. Reflect on the Bible's assurance that the Holy Spirit intercedes for you when you pray. How does this truth affect your understanding of prayer?

3. God has given His Spirit as our Helper and Guide. What do these verses teach us about how to pray?

Ephesians 6:18

Jude 20-21

4. The Scriptures emphasize praying in the Spirit. What are some ways in which we quench the Holy Spirit in our prayer life?

> When we are born again of God and are indwelt by the Spirit of God, He expresses for us the unutterable. "He," the Spirit in you, "maketh intercession for the saints according to the will of God," and God searches your heart not to know what your conscious prayers are, but to find out what is the prayer of the Holy Spirit. The Spirit of God needs the nature of the believer as a shrine in which to offer His intercession.[4]
>
> OSWALD CHAMBERS

5. Paul affirms to the Corinthians God's desire to richly bless those who love Him. Read 1 Corinthians 2:9-16 and record your observations on the work of the Holy Spirit in our lives.

6. Another help God has given to us is His Word, which is inspired by the Holy Spirit. Read John 15:7 and write down the conditions of answered prayer.

7. "To abide in Christ," writes R. A. Torrey, "is to renounce any independent life of our own."[5] Why do you think God so closely intertwines our abiding in Him, His Word, and answered prayer?

> To sum it all up, if you want that splendid power in prayer, you must remain in loving, living, lasting, conscious, practical, abiding union with the Lord Jesus Christ. . . . So be filled with God's Word. Study what Jesus has said, what the Holy Ghost has left on record in this divinely inspired book, and in proportion as you feed on, retain, and obey the Word in your life, you will be a master in the art of prayer.[6]
> CHARLES SPURGEON

AUTHOR'S REFLECTION

If I am abiding—spending time alone with God and His Word—then my heart is being trained to ask for the eternal things of God. My heart becomes set on "things above, not on the things that are on earth." As I ask for that which is eternal, I begin to pray in the Spirit, according to the will of God and on the strong foundation of Scripture.

It has been a discipline of mine over the years to pray Scripture into the fabric of my life. At the beginning of each year I ask the Lord what He wants to accomplish in my life for the next twelve months. As I listen and am sensitive to the Spirit and my Scripture reading, a need or a verse of Scripture is brought to my mind. When the verse or verses are chosen, I make a bookmark with the Scripture written on it. I cover it with clear contact paper, memorize it, and put it in my Bible. Then every day I pray over the verse and ask God to make His Word part of my life.

I can give you a history of my life by the verses I have memorized! One year I chose Micah 6:8. I needed to begin to learn humility and that was the year God faithfully and graciously allowed me to be in several situations where humility could have a tiny beginning as part of my character. Another year God seemed to highlight Hebrews 12:1 for me. All that year I asked the Lord to show me how to lay aside the weights in my life, to be aware of the sin that could so easily entangle me, and to teach me to endure the race set before me. Praying and meditating over that verse changed my life. God answered my prayers by showing me that people pleasing was a great hindrance in my life. Psalm 141:4 was brought to my attention and I realized that I easily ate around the delicacies of sin. God also taught me that if I am to endure the race, I must pace myself.

Our gracious God gives us His Spirit to undergird us in prayer. How privileged we are to seek His help in confidence that He will guide us to pray according to His Word.

> Indeed the whole secret of prayer is found in these three words, *in the Spirit*. It is the prayer that God the Holy Spirit inspires that God the Father answers. . . . The one who would pray in the Spirit must meditate much upon the Word, that the Holy Spirit may have something through which He can work. The Holy Spirit works His prayers in us through the Word, and neglect of the Word makes praying in the Holy Spirit an impossibility. If we would feed the fire of our prayers with the fuel of God's Word, all our difficulties in prayer would disappear.[7]
>
> R. A. TORREY

A Prayer Concerning God's Help

David acknowledges God's help in Psalm 138. In your time with the Lord, pray this prayer. Add your own thoughts concerning your need for praying in the Spirit and abiding in His Word.

DAVID'S PRAYER

I will bow down toward Thy holy temple,
And give thanks to Thy name for Thy lovingkindness
  and Thy truth;
For Thou hast magnified Thy word according to all
  Thy name.
On the day I called Thou didst answer me;
Thou didst make me bold with strength in my soul.
(Psalm 138:2-3)

MY PRAYER

Suggested Scripture Memory
Romans 8:26

CHAPTER FOUR

DELIGHTING IN GOD

Delight yourself in the LORD;
And He will give you the desires of your heart.
PSALM 37:4

Men who delight in God desire or ask
for nothing but what will please God;
hence it is safe to give them carte blanche.
Their will is subdued to God's will,
and now they may have what they will.
Our innermost desires are here meant,
not our casual wishes;
there are many things which nature might desire
which grace would never permit us to ask for;
these deep, prayerful, asking desires
are those to which the promise is made.[1]
CHARLES SPURGEON

If I delight myself in the Lord, He will give me the desires of my heart. What a great verse; what a wonderful promise! If I truly love God and tell Him the desires of my heart, then I will have whatever I want—isn't that what the verse says? If it is, then why doesn't it work? At least, He should grant my good, godly desires! This is a question that I have struggled with for a long time, as have many others. What does this verse really mean? How does my *delighting* ensure that God will grant my desires? It is essential that as we consider how to become a woman of prayer, we understand what it means to delight ourselves in the Lord.

Prayer of Preparation

As you begin this chapter, pray with Amy Carmichael (twentieth century) for an understanding of what it is to delight yourself in the Lord:

> That which I know not teach Thou me.
> Who, blessed Lord, teacheth like Thee?
> Lead my desires that they may be
>   According to Thy will.[2]

Our Delight in God

1. God asks us to delight ourselves in Him. What does *delight* mean? (Use a dictionary to help create your own definition.)

2. It is important to God that we delight ourselves in Him. Read the verses below and record your thoughts about what is necessary to take delight in the Lord.

Nehemiah 1:11

Psalm 1:1-3

Psalm 40:8

Psalm 111:2

Jeremiah 15:16

---

3. Summarize these Scriptures by writing down the characteristics of someone who delights herself in the Lord.

> Initially, I responded to His call to delight in Him to ensure the fulfillment of His promise to give me the desires of my heart. I had no idea that He would give me a new heart (Jer. 24:7). I didn't know that He would begin working in me to reproduce His own heart. When I turned to Him, I found that He Himself is my very great reward (Gen. 15:1). He is not, as I had supposed, the means to my end. Instead He is the desire of my heart.[3]
> JENNIFER KENNEDY DEAN

God's Delight in Our Prayers

4. In Isaiah 66:4 God speaks sternly to those who "chose that in which I did not delight." Study the following verses and write down under the appropriate column the choices that please Him and those that do not please Him.

What Delights God	What Does Not Delight God
1 Samuel 15:20-22	
Proverbs 11:20	

34

What Delights God	What Does Not Delight God
Proverbs 15:8	
Hosea 6:6	

5. Based on your study of the passages above, write out your thoughts about why the qualities that God delights in are key for an intimate prayer life with Him.

> We may be sure that, as we delight in what God
> delights in, such prayer is inspired by God and will have
> its answer. And our prayer becomes unceasingly,
> "Thy desires, O my Father, are mine. Thy holy will
> of love is my will too."[4]
> ANDREW MURRAY

AUTHOR'S REFLECTION

Sometimes I am a little hesitant to pray specifically for certain things I want. I always want to be sure that I am praying according to the will of God and not from my own selfish desires.

I think of the Israelites in the wilderness who prayed for meat. This does not seem to be an inappropriate request, yet it shows their discontent with God. Psalm 78:18 says, "And in their heart they put God to the test by asking food according to *their desire*" (emphasis added). Certainly these people were not delighting in God. They were rebellious and didn't believe God; they chose that in which He did not delight. "So He gave them their request, but sent a wasting disease among them" (Psalm 106:15).

I want to be sure that I am delighting in God's Word, that I am reverencing His name, and that I am walking in obedience. For when my heart is set on walking blamelessly before the Lord, then my delight is only in what He wills. Psalm 145:19 tells us, "He will fulfill the desire of those who fear Him. . . ." And Psalm 78:18 tells us that sometimes God will fulfill the desire of those who test Him!

There is certainly nothing wrong with letting God know our desire, but it needs to be shared in the context of His will. The Lord, in His prayer to the Father, clearly stated His desire for the cup to be taken from Him. He went on to say, though, "yet not My will, but Thine be done" (Luke 22:42). I like Spurgeon's prayer, "Lord, if what I ask for does not please You, neither would it please me. My desires are put into Your hands to be corrected. Strike the pen through every petition that I offer that is not right. And put in whatever I have omitted, even though I might not have desired it had I considered it. . . . 'Not as I will, but as Thou wilt.'"[5]

36

One of my favorite verses of Scripture is, "Whom have I in heaven but You? And I have no delight or desire on earth beside You" (Psalm 73:25, AMP). I want to focus on what pleases God, not on what pleases myself. This is the cry of my heart—that I would have no delight or desire on earth besides the Lord.

> What is the desire of the heart of a good man?
> It is this, to know, and love, and live to God,
> to please him and to be pleased in him.[6]
> MATTHEW HENRY

A Prayer to Delight in the Lord
Asaph beautifully expresses his heart for God and God alone. Confirm with the Lord your desire to delight only in Him by praying this prayer. You may want to add your own thoughts to Asaph's prayer.

ASAPH'S PRAYER
Whom have I in heaven but You?
And I have no delight or desire on earth beside You.
My flesh and my heart may fail, but God is the rock
and firm strength of my heart, and my portion for ever.
(Psalm 73:25-26, AMP)

MY PRAYER

Suggested Scripture Memory
Psalm 37:4

CHAPTER FIVE

GOD'S ANSWERS

I sought the LORD, and He answered me,
And delivered me from all my fears.
PSALM 34:4

I think we sometimes discourage ourselves
by a misconception of the exact meaning of the
expression, "answer," taking it to mean only
grant. Now, an answer is not necessarily
an acquiescence. It may be a refusal,
an explanation, a promise, a conditional grant.
It is, in fact, simply attention to our request
expressed. In this sense, before we call he will
answer, and while we are yet speaking
he will hear [Isaiah 65:24].[1]
MARY B. M. DUNCAN

D avid testifies that as he called upon the Lord, He answered him. God's immediate answer for David's predicament was to deliver him from all his *fears*, not from his trouble! Jeremiah 33:3 tells us that if we call to God, He will answer. God does answer, but He does not always respond in the way we think He should. The response we all want from God is "Yes!" But God's answers also include "No," "Wait," and "Trust." That is why it is vital that our prayers are not demanding, but offered in faith and in the Spirit with delight in the Lord, His Word, and His will. Understanding that God has His ways of answering our prayers is essential to prevailing prayer. Grasping the importance of releasing the answers to our prayers to a sovereign, loving God is key to becoming a woman of prayer.

Prayer of Preparation

As you begin this chapter, pray with Saint Ignatius of Loyola (sixteenth century) that God Himself is answer enough for all you need.

> Take, O Lord, and receive my entire liberty, my memory, my understanding, and my whole will. All that I am, all that I have, you have given me and I will give it back again to you to be disposed of according to your good pleasure. Give me only your love and your grace; with you I am rich enough, nor do I ask for aught besides. Amen.[2]

God's Gifts in Prayer

1. When Jesus taught on prayer, He used a parable to encourage us that the Father will answer. As you read Luke 11:5-13, answer the following questions.

   a. What should characterize our prayers? (verses 5-10)

b. How does Jesus picture the Father's response?
(verses 11-13)

Spiritual lust makes me demand an answer from God,
instead of seeking God Who gives the answer. . . .
The meaning of prayer is that we get hold of God,
not the answer.[3]
OSWALD CHAMBERS

---

2. A key Scripture on prayer is found in Philippians. Read
Philippians 4:6-7 and write down what Paul teaches
regarding our prayer and God's answers.

a. How we are to pray (verse 6)

b. How God answers (verse 7)

> We think that we understand better than He does when
> and how our prayers should be answered. . . . We make
> use of prayer to convince God that we see the matter in
> the right light, that the answer should be given
> immediately, and should be as we have planned it. . . .
> We are afraid that God will not permit Himself to be
> convinced by our prayer, but will do as He wills
> regardless of our supplications. . . . When, therefore, the
> Spirit has taught us that God is inexorable on this point
> and that He Himself decides when and how our prayers
> are to be answered, then we shall experience rest
> and peace when we pray.[4]
> O. HALLESBY

3. From the passages of Scripture you studied in the previous
   questions, record your thoughts concerning what God
   considers important in answering prayer.

4. Throughout the Bible, we can find many examples of God's responses to His people when they prayed. Read the following passages. For each one, write down the request made and the answer God gave.

a. Abraham asked his servant, Eliezer, to find a bride for Isaac. Read Eliezer's prayer in Genesis 24:12-20 and record how God answered.

The Request	The Answer

b. God appeared to Solomon in a dream and asked him to tell Him what he wanted. Read about Solomon's request and God's answer in 1 Kings 3:3-14.

The Request	The Answer

c. Martha and Mary called Jesus when their brother, Lazarus, was sick. Read in John 11:1-6 how Jesus responded.

The Request	The Answer

d. Paul was given a thorn in the flesh. Read 2 Corinthians 12:7-10. What was his prayer, and what did God say to him?

The Request	The Answer

We all tend to prescribe the answers to our prayers. We think that God can come in only one way. But Scripture teaches us that God sometimes answers our prayers by allowing things to become much worse before they become better. He may sometimes do the opposite of what we anticipate. . . . Yet it is a fundamental principle in the life and walk of faith that we must always be prepared for the unexpected when we are dealing with God.[5]
D. MARTYN LLOYD-JONES

5. Jesus prayed to the Father about going to the cross. Read the account in Luke's Gospel (22:39-46) to discover Jesus' request and the Father's answer.

The Request	The Answer

44

From all false ideas the history of this prayer of Christ
delivers us. It is a precious lesson of the Cross that
apparent failure is eternal victory. It is a precious lesson
of this prayer that the object of prayer is not the success
of its petition, nor is its rejection a proof of failure.
Christ's petition was not gratified, yet He was the one
well-beloved of His Father.

All prayer is to change the human will into submission
to the divine will "as thou wilt." . . . Practically then, I
say, Pray as He did, until prayer makes you cease praying.
Pray until prayer makes you forget your own wish, and
leave it or merge it in God's will. The divine wisdom has
given us prayer, not as a means whereby we escape evil,
but as a means whereby we become strong to meet it.
"There appeared an angel unto Him from heaven,
strengthening Him" [Luke 22:43]. That was
the true reply to His prayer.[6]
FREDERICK W. ROBERTSON

AUTHOR'S REFLECTION

Certainly God does answer prayer. He answers in His way, in
His time, for our good and His glory. Since this is true, then
why do we need to pray? For more than twenty years I have
kept a newsletter from Richard Halverson that helped to answer
that question for me. Here is part of what he wrote, "God will
not rule without the consent of those over whom He rules! God
is neither Tyrant or Paternalist! . . . And this is the point of
prayer. By prayer man consents to the rule of God in his life. By
prayer man seeks God's will and yields to it. By prayer man asks
God for that which he knows he needs and can receive only
from God. . . . Prayer is that contact man has with the Heavenly
Father to satisfy the deepest needs of his life."[7]

D. L. Moody used to say that he thanked God with all his
heart that many of his most earnest prayers had not been
granted! It can be exciting to pray and then watch how God
answers. How quickly God answered Eliezer; how generous
He was to Solomon; what an incredible experience for Martha
and Mary to see Lazarus raised from the dead; what humility

Paul learned from his thorn. God so desires to bless above and beyond what we could ask or think, to give the eternal, to strengthen us, to show us great and unsearchable things that can come only by prayer.

Once when I was diligently interceding by asking, seeking, and knocking, what I was given was peace, what I found was the ability to persevere and to trust, and what was opened was a deepened intimacy with the Lord. My request has yet to be fully granted, but my prayer has been fully answered.

This leads to a very old question: does prayer influence God? No question has been discussed more, or more earnestly. Skeptical men of fine scientific training have with great positiveness said "no," and Christian men of scholarly training and strong faith have with equal positiveness said "yes." Not right in all their statements, nor right in all their beliefs, nor right in all their processes of thinking, but right in their ultimate conclusions as represented by these short words, "no," and "yes." Prayer does not influence God. Prayer surely does influence God. It does not influence His purpose. It does influence His action. Everything that ever has been prayed for, of course I mean every right thing, God has already purposed to do. But He does nothing without our consent. He has been hindered in His purposes by our lack of willingness. When we learn His purposes and make them our prayers we are giving Him the opportunity to act.[8]

S. D. GORDON

Prayer for Trust in God's Answers

David expresses his trust in God's ability to answer according to His lovingkindness. Pray this prayer with David and add your own prayer for perseverance that recognizes God's answers.

DAVID'S PRAYER

But as for me, my prayer is to Thee, O LORD, at an acceptable time;

46

O God, in the greatness of Thy lovingkindness,
Answer me with Thy saving truth.
(Psalm 69:13)

Suggested Scripture Memory
Psalm 34:4

CHAPTER SIX

WHEN GOD IS SILENT

But to You I cry, O Lord;
and in the morning shall my prayer
come to meet You.
Lord, why do You cast me off?
Why do You hide Your face from me?
PSALM 88:13-14, AMP

We may experience times of unusual closeness,
when every prayer is answered in an obvious
way and God seems intimate and caring.
And we may also experience "fog times,"
when God stays silent, when nothing
works according to formula and
all the Bible's promises seem glaringly false.
Fidelity involves learning to trust that,
out beyond the perimeter of fog,
God still reigns and has not abandoned us,
no matter how it appears.[1]
PHILIP YANCEY

Many of us have felt like Hemen, the psalmist. We pray and there is nothing. Has God heard? Will He answer? Will He respond in some way to me? To be silent is to be uncommunicative, passive. Silence can also mean quiet and calm. We need to know how we should react when there is seemingly no response from the Lord. God has been clear in His Word about what He can and cannot hear. It is necessary to study what causes God to turn away from us. It is also good to remember that we cannot know the mind of the Lord, for His ways are unfathomable and His judgments are unsearchable.

Prayer of Preparation

As you begin to study, pray with Benjamin Jenks (seventeenth century) for understanding of God's dealings with us.

> Oh, teach us to know you, our God, and enable us to do your will as we ought to do. Give us hearts to love you, to trust and delight in you. That no temptations may draw us, nor any tribulations drive us from you; but that all your dispensations to us, and all your dealings with us, may be the messengers of your love to our souls, to bring us still nearer to your blessed self, and to make us still fitter for your heavenly kingdom.[2]

Silence and Conviction of Sin

1. Our God invites us to pray, but sometimes it appears that He does not reply. The Scriptures tell us the reasons God may be silent. Study the verses given and write down the hindrances to answered prayer.

   Psalm 66:18

Proverbs 21:13

Proverbs 28:9

Ezekiel 14:3

Matthew 5:23-24

James 4:1-3

2. "Only give heed to yourself and keep your soul diligently" (Deuteronomy 4:9) is good instruction in light of the verses in question 1. What key areas of our lives do we need to "give heed to" in order to ensure that God hears our prayers?

> Anyone who finds his prayers ineffective should not conclude that the thing which he asks of God is not according to His will, but should go alone with God with the psalmist's prayer, "Search me, O God, and know my heart: try me, and know my thoughts: and see if there be any wicked way in me" (Psalm 139:23-24), and wait before Him until He puts His finger upon the thing that is displeasing in His sight. Then this sin should be confessed and put away.[3]
> R. A. TORREY

Silence and Deeper Intimacy

3. Job was an expert on God's silence. Job was righteous, yet God allowed Satan to afflict him. Job then cried out to God for an answer, but for a time all he received was silence. Read the following verses and discover how God worked.

   a. How did Job express his complaint to God? (Job 30:16-20)

b. When God did finally speak to Job, how did Job respond? (Job 40:1-5)

c. After God spoke the second time, Job answered the Lord. Explain how you think Job's prayer life and relationship to God changed after that experience. (Job 42:1-6)

4. Job went through a hard school of suffering and a difficult season of God's silence. What can you learn from Job's experience for your own prayer life?

Some prayers are followed by silence because they are wrong, others because they are bigger than we can understand. Jesus stayed where He was—a positive staying, because He loved Martha and Mary. Did they get Lazarus back? They got infinitely more; they got to know the greatest truth mortal beings ever knew—that Jesus Christ is the Resurrection and the Life. It will be a wonderful moment when we stand before God and find that the prayers we clamored for in early days and imagined were never answered, have been answered in the most amazing way, and that God's silence has been the sign of the answer. If we always want to be able to point to something and say, "This is the way God answered my prayer," God cannot trust us yet with His silence.[4]

OSWALD CHAMBERS

AUTHOR'S REFLECTION

Proverbs 15:8 tells us, "But the prayer of the upright is His delight." When I feel that my prayers are just "hitting the ceiling" and I don't think that God is listening, it is good that I can go to the Lord and ask Him to pinpoint any sin in my life. He is very faithful to respond! Often He brings to mind my transgression. I confess it and am cleansed from all unrighteousness. Then my prayer is one in which He can take delight.

But then there are times when I feel God is silent and I go to Him and I receive no word that I am hindering prayer, but what I do sense is His presence, that He is with me, and that I am to trust Him for His way and His timing. In a way, I am to be silent in His silence. These have been precious times to me—to know that He is with me, and that is enough.

"The period of waiting for the granting of some request," says Lloyd John Ogilvie, "is often rewarded by a far greater gift than what we asked for. The Lord Himself. . . . The purpose of unanswered prayer is to lead us from hearsay to heartsight. Job could say, 'I have heard of You by the hearing of the ear, but now my eye sees You.'"[5]

It is possible that some who read these words may have a complaint against God. A controversy of long-standing has come between your soul and His grace. If you were to utter the word that is trembling on your lips, you would say to Him, "Why hast Thou dealt thus with me?" Then dare to say, with reverence and with boldness, all that is in your heart. "Produce your cause, saith the Lord; bring forth your strong reasons, saith the King of Jacob" ([Isaiah 41:21]). Carry your grievance into the light of His countenance; charge your complaint home. Then listen to His answer. For surely, in gentleness and truth, He will clear Himself of the charge of unkindness that you bring against Him. And in His light you shall see light. But, remember that this is a private matter between you and your Lord, and you must not defame Him to any one.[6]

DAVID M'INTYRE

Prayer of Trusting in God

Trusting God sometimes means learning to rest in His silence. To quiet your heart in trust, pray this passage of David's and then add your own prayer.

DAVID'S PRAYER

My soul, wait in silence for God only,
For my hope is from Him.
He only is my rock and my salvation,
My stronghold; I shall not be shaken.
(Psalm 62:5-6)

MY PRAYER

Suggested Scripture Memory
Psalm 88:13-14

CHAPTER SEVEN

THE LORD'S PATTERN OF PRAYER

I love the LORD, because He hears
My voice and my supplications.
Because He has inclined His ear to me,
Therefore I shall call upon Him
as long as I live.
PSALM 116:1-2

Whether we praise him for his unfathomable
majesty or petition him for daily needs,
prayer is the expression of our dependence
upon God, our whole-souled reliance
upon his power to sustain us,
his mercy to forgive us,
his bounty to supply us,
and his glory to overwhelm us
as we reflect on who he is.[1]
C. SAMUEL STORMS

God desires communion with us. He invites us, and He provides help for us through His Word and His Spirit. We must have faith, delight ourselves in Him and His will, and trust in His ways to pray effectively. But when we do finally come to the Lord, what do we say? How do we pray? Can we pray for our own needs? We are not alone in asking these questions. The disciples, who began to observe Jesus' vital prayer life, asked Jesus to teach them to pray, and Jesus graciously answered their request and ours.

Prayer of Preparation
As you begin this chapter, pray with John Wesley (eighteenth century) for your own heart to be strengthened in Him.

Take the full possession of my heart, raise there your throne, and command there as you do in heaven. Being created by you, let me live to you. Being created for you, let me ever act for your glory. Being redeemed by you, let me render unto you what is yours, and let my spirit ever cleave to you alone.[2]

A Model Prayer
Jesus answered the disciples' request by giving them a comprehensive pattern of prayer. Carefully study and meditate on Matthew 6:9-15. (The traditional form of the Lord's Prayer is used in the following questions; some Bible versions bracket or footnote the final phrase.)

---

1. "Our Father"—What do you think is the significance of this opening address?

2. "Who art in heaven"—Why do you think it's important that we acknowledge that He is in heaven?

3. "Hallowed be Thy name"—Define the word *hallowed* and how it applies to our heavenly Father.

4. "Thy kingdom come, Thy will be done, on earth as it is in heaven"—Rephrase this petition as an expression of your desire to participate in its fulfillment.

5. "Give us this day our daily bread"—What do you think "daily bread" means, and why are we to ask for it one day at a time?

6. "And forgive us our debts, as we also have forgiven our debtors" (see also verses 14-15)—Why do you think Jesus links God's forgiveness of us with our forgiveness of others?

7. "And do not lead us into temptation, but deliver us from evil"—Rewrite this petition in your own words.

I was never worried myself by the words *lead us not into temptation*, but a great many of my correspondents are. The words suggest to them what someone has called "a fiend-like conception of God," as one who first forbids us certain fruits and then lures us to taste them. But the Greek word . . . means "trial"—"trying circumstances"— of every sort; a far larger word than English "temptation." So that the petition essentially is "Make straight our paths. Spare us, where possible, from all crises, whether of temptation or affliction." . . . "In my ignorance I have asked for A, B, and C. But don't give me them if you foresee that they would in reality be to me either snares or sorrows." . . . If God had granted all the silly prayers I've made in my life, where should I be now?[3]

C. S. LEWIS

8. "For Thine is the kingdom, and the power, and the glory, forever. Amen"—Look back over the preceding phrases you have just studied. How does this closing statement sum up the Lord's Prayer?

9. This prayer model given by Jesus is brief but profound. How would you summarize the key characteristics or elements of this model that provide a pattern for how God desires us to pray?

> But the great beauty of the Lord's Prayer
> is that it maintains a focus on God. We may be the
> grammatical object of some sentences there, but we are
> never the subject; God alone holds that position. Even in
> confession, we turn our eyes to Him and say, "*You* give us
> bread . . . *You* forgive us . . . *You* lead us . . . *You* deliver
> us." That kind of prayer provides us with an oft-needed
> corrective. For perhaps the most subtle temptation,
> the most persistent evil of all is to stand ourselves
> in God's rightful place at the center of the
> landscape of our hearts.[4]
> PAUL THIGPEN

Father, thank You for this prayer that is concise, yet also so expansive. You have given the perfect outline to follow and to build upon. I no longer have to wonder, *How shall I pray?*

Prayer is best when I am alone with You and undistracted. How special that You desire secret communion with me. What freedom You give me, for You already know my needs, so I don't have to go into a lot of detail to fill You in!

I'm glad that You are *our* Father. It helps me to remember to pray for others, to recall that I am not alone in my struggles or my praise. Although You are sovereign, majestic, and in heaven where I know that You reign, You are also our *Father*. You love me and care for me; I am Your child. I can dwell on that for a long time. You are holy and I come to You in great reverence and awe. Your kingdom being established here on earth needs to be a burning concern of mine as I pray and as I live. Wanting Your will and Your glory to be evidenced in our world begins with me.

Father, You made so clear what are the most important things I need to ask You for. Thank You that I can ask You simply and directly for my everyday needs. You don't want me to be apprehensive about future provision. You desire that I take one day at a time. Always, I am to come before You confessing my sin and being sure that I have a clear conscience before You and others. No matter what I go through, Lord, keep me pure, steadfast, and protected from evil. I am weak and I need You. For it is Your kingdom, and Your power, and Your glory that I desire to uphold.

> In this prayer Jesus laid down the principles
> governing man's relationship to God, and these are
> relevant to believers in every age. It should be noted that
> He did not say, "Pray in these precise words," but "Pray,
> then, in this way" (v. 9). He was giving a pattern, not an
> inflexible form. The exact words employed may vary
> greatly, while the individual prayer itself conforms
> to the pattern given.[5]
> J. OSWALD SANDERS

A Prayer of Adoration

David praises and petitions God continually throughout his life.
Pray this prayer of his, and add your own prayer for an appropriate attitude or posture as you come before God to pray.

DAVID'S PRAYER

Thy kingdom is an everlasting kingdom,
And Thy dominion endures throughout all generations.

The LORD sustains all who fall,
And raises up all who are bowed down.
The eyes of all look to Thee,
And Thou dost give them their food in due time.
(Psalm 145:13-15)

MY PRAYER

Suggested Scripture Memory
Psalm 116:1-2

CHAPTER EIGHT

INTERCESSORY PRAYER

*Make this your common practice: Confess your
sins to each other and pray for each other
so that you can live together whole and healed.
The prayer of a person living right with God
is something powerful to be reckoned with.*
JAMES 5:16, MSG

*Beware of imagining that intercession
means bringing our personal sympathies into
the presence of God and demanding that He
does what we ask. Our approach to God is due
entirely to the vicarious identification of our
Lord with sin. We have "boldness to enter into
the holiest by the blood of Jesus.". . . Vicarious
intercession means that we deliberately
substitute God's interests in others for our
natural sympathy with them.*[1]
OSWALD CHAMBERS

The Lord's Prayer teaches us to pray *our* and *us*. Intercession is woven into the fabric of Jesus' teaching on prayer. We are told in Romans 8:27 and 8:34 that the Holy Spirit and Christ Jesus intercede for us. Intercession is precious to the heart of God. To intercede means to plead on behalf of someone. If we are abiding in Him and His desires are our desires, then we cannot help but be concerned about others. Our family, our church, our friends, our neighbors, our enemies, our world, our leaders all need our prayers. I so appreciate the way Paul commended Epaphras to the Colossians: "always laboring earnestly for you in his prayers, that you may stand perfect and fully assured in all the will of God" (Colossians 4:12). It is a privilege to labor earnestly for others.

Prayer of Preparation

As you begin this chapter pray with Saint Polycarp (first–second centuries) for a heart to intercede.

> May God the Father, and the eternal high priest Jesus Christ, build us up in faith and truth and love, and grant to us our portion among the saints with all those who believe on our Lord Jesus Christ. We pray for all saints, for kings and rulers, for the enemies of the cross of Christ, and for ourselves we pray that our fruit may abound and we may be made perfect in Christ Jesus our Lord. Amen.[2]

An Equipped Intercessor

1. James states that "The effective prayer of a righteous man can accomplish much" (5:16). Study Ephesians 6:10-18 and record your answers to the following questions.

   a. Where is our strength? (verse 10)

b. Why is the armor of God necessary? (verses 11-12)

c. What is the armor of God? (verses 14-17)

d. What are we to do once we have put on the full armor? (verse 18)

---

2. As you reflect on your study of this passage in Ephesians, record your thoughts regarding why we need to put on the armor of God in order to pray.

That word *praying* is the climax of this long sentence, and of this whole epistle [Ephesians]. This is the sort of action that turns the enemy's flank, and reveals his heels. He simply *cannot* stand before persistent knee-work.

Now mark the keenness of Paul's description of the man who does his most effective work in praying. There are six qualifications under the figure of the six pieces of armour. A clear understanding of truth, a clean obedient life, earnest service, a strongly simple trust in God, clear assurance of one's own salvation and relation to God, and a good grip of the truth for others—these things prepare a man for the real conflict of prayer. *Such a man— praying—drives back these hosts of the traitor prince.* Such a man praying is invincible in his Chief, Jesus.[3]

S. D. GORDON

A Committed Intercessor

3. Paul's desire was to intercede for the church. Read these prayers and choose one you would like to begin using for someone on your prayer list: Ephesians 3:14-21, Colossians 1:9-12, 2 Thessalonians 1:11-12. Next to the person's name, write down the major petitions in this prayer.

> Paul did not pray that they be spared suffering.
> Nor did he request that material wealth be added to their
> spiritual zeal. He said nothing about illness, or healing,
> or better jobs, or any of those things for which we pray
> and ask others to pray on our behalf. Such requests are
> not always inappropriate, but we see that Paul considered
> spiritual wisdom, knowledge, and enlightenment
> of greater value.[4]
> C. SAMUEL STORMS

4. Scripture teaches us to pray for nations and governing
   authorities. What can you learn from the following passages about how we are to pray for our world?

   2 Chronicles 7:11-16

   1 Timothy 2:1-2

5. Jesus' high priestly prayer is a beautiful example of intercession. Read through His prayer in John 17, and write down your impressions concerning His requests for the disciples and for all believers.

6. It is a privilege to labor earnestly in intercessory prayer. What would you like to change or strengthen in the way you pray for others?

AUTHOR'S REFLECTION

One day I was feeling somewhat depressed. I prayed and asked the Lord what the cause might be, but I did not receive a specific answer. A little while later, the sadness lifted and I asked the Lord, "What happened?" Immediately, in my heart, I heard this thought: *Someone just prayed for you.*

"Lord, make me sensitive to the promptings of Your Holy Spirit" is a constant prayer of mine. Whenever someone is laid on my heart or brought to my mind, I need to be an intercessor. Often I don't know exactly what to pray and that is why it is good to study Paul's prayers and the Lord's prayer in John 17. I have taken some of Jesus' requests and I pray them for my family and for others when I'm not sure of the need. I pray that they would know God, be kept in His name, be kept from the evil one, and be sanctified in the truth.

I have also found it helpful to pray specific Scripture for others. As I know the need, I find prayers, psalms, or verses that speak to their situation. For example, for someone who has turned away from the Lord I pray 2 Timothy 2:25-26— "if perhaps God may grant them repentance leading to the knowledge of the truth, and they may come to their senses and escape from the snare of the devil, having been held captive by him to do his will."

How little we realize what impact our intercession has in the kingdom of God. God is gracious to give us the privilege of prayer that allows us to participate with Him in ministering to others.

One of the earliest lessons we learned together was that before asking for anything we should find out if it were according to the mind of the Lord. This . . . intercession needed preparation of a special kind. It needed time — time to listen, to understand, to "wait.". . . And this is the confidence that we have in Him that *if we ask anything according to His will He heareth us:* and if we know that He hears us whatsoever we ask, *we know that we have* the petitions that we desired of Him. The more we pondered over all that is said about prayer in the only book in the world that can speak with authority about it, the more we found to make us ask to be filled with the knowledge of His will before offering petitions for a desired good. When we were in doubt about His will (as we often were and are) and had not liberty to ask for a clear sign, there was the prayer of prayers ready framed for us: Thy will be done, whatever that will may be. But when we are meant to know our Lord's wishes, we must be shown what they are before we can lay our prayer alongside, and often our first prayer was for spiritual understanding and direction in prayer.[7]
AMY CARMICHAEL

A Prayer to Be an Equipped and Committed Intercessor
God spoke in Ezekiel saying, "And I searched for a man among them who should build up the wall and stand in the gap before Me for the land, that I should not destroy it; but I found no one" (Ezekiel 22:30). Often the Lord is looking for someone to "stand in the gap" in prayer. Join with Samuel in resolving to be that one, and add your own prayer expressing your desire to be a faithful intercessor.

A PRAYER OF RESOLVE

As for me, far be it from me that I should sin against the LORD by ceasing to pray for you. (1 Samuel 12:23)

MY PRAYER

Suggested Scripture Memory
James 5:16

CHAPTER NINE

PERSEVERING IN PRAYER

*Be earnest and unwearied and steadfast
in your prayer [life], being [both] alert and
intent in [your praying] with thanksgiving.*
COLOSSIANS 4:2, AMP

*When we feel least like praying is the time
when we most need to pray. We should wait
quietly before God and tell Him how cold and
prayerless our hearts are, and look up to Him
and trust Him and expect Him to send the Holy
Spirit to warm our hearts and draw them out
in prayer. It will not be long before the glow
of the Spirit's presence will fill our hearts,
and we will begin to pray with freedom,
directness, earnestness and power.*[1]
R. A. TORREY

P aul asks the Colossians to *devote* themselves to prayer. One who is devoted is faithful, untiring, persistent, and persevering. In our devotion to prayer, we are instructed to stay alert in our praying by having an attitude of thanksgiving. Persevering in prayer and praise is essential if we are to become women of prayer. It is hard to keep praying when we don't feel like praying, and it is certainly difficult to praise God when we are not praying! Devotion not only involves discipline to continue praying, but it also implies persistence and patience in waiting for answers to our prayers. Praise and thanksgiving are an essential part of persevering prayer. The more we focus on praising God, the more devoted and faithful we become.

Prayer of Preparation

As you begin this chapter, pray with George Herbert (seventeenth century) that God will lead you into a life of continuous praise:

> Thou hast given so much to me,
> Give one thing more—a grateful heart;
> Not thankful when it pleaseth me,
> As if Thy blessings had spare days,
> But such a heart whose pulse may be
> Thy praise.[2]

Devotion to Prayer

1. "Pray, and don't faint" are words Jesus used to teach about the importance of persevering in prayer. Read the parable in Luke 18:1-8 and write down Jesus' teaching about prevailing in prayer.

> Since God is a loving heavenly Father who knows
> all our needs better than we do, why should He require
> us to importune Him? Why does He not just grant our
> requests, as He is well able to do?
>
> This is somewhat of a mystery, and the answer
> does not appear on the surface. We can be assured that
> there is no reluctance on God's part to give us whatever is
> good for us. He does not need to be coaxed, for He is not
> capricious. Prayer is not a means of extorting blessing
> from unwilling fingers. . . . The answer must be sought
> elsewhere. The necessity must lie in us, not in God.
> It is not God who is under test, but our own
> spiritual maturity.[3]
> J. OSWALD SANDERS

2. It may seem puzzling to continue offering the same
   request again and again. Why do you think God wants us
   to keep petitioning Him?

3. Hannah is a beautiful example of devoted prayer. Read
   1 Samuel 1:1-18 and describe her situation and persistence.

> [T]he strong man of prayer when he starts to pray for a
> thing keeps on praying until he prays it through, and
> obtains what he seeks. We should be careful about what
> we ask from God, but when we do begin to pray for a
> thing we should never give up praying for it until we get
> it, or until God makes it very clear and very definite to us
> that it is not His will to give it.[4]
> R. A. TORREY

Gratitude in Prayer

4. God, because He is not an unjust judge, answered
   Hannah's fervent, steadfast prayer. Read her prayer of
   exultation and record her specific praise of God's
   character. (1 Samuel 2:1-10)

> What great things she says of God. She takes little
> notice of the particular mercy she was now rejoicing in,
> does not commend Samuel for the prettiest child, the
> most toward and sensible for his age that she ever saw, as
> fond parents are too apt to do. No, she overlooks the gift
> and praises the giver; whereas most forget the giver and
> fasten only on the gift. Every stream should lead us to
> the fountain; and the favours we receive from God
> should raise our admiration of the infinite
> perfections there are in God.[5]
> MATTHEW HENRY

5. Thanksgiving is an integral part of prayer. Study these verses and write a paragraph on why you think we are to be thankful when we pray: Philippians 4:6-7; Colossians 3:16-17, 4:2.

6. God proclaims, "The people whom I formed for Myself, will declare My praise" (Isaiah 43:21). Praise is joyful, thankful, worshipful prayer. Read Psalm 146 and write down what the psalmist praised God for.

> Praise and thanksgiving do not magically
> change my circumstances. They radically alter my
> viewpoint. Praise and thanksgiving bring me back into
> the presence of God, where there is fullness of joy
> and pleasures evermore.[6]
> JENNIFER KENNEDY DEAN

AUTHOR'S REFLECTION

Knowing that the Lord does not wish for any to perish, but for all to come to repentance (2 Peter 3:9), I began to pray for my father's salvation. I prayed fairly consistently for twenty-three years. I kept telling the Lord that my dad would make such a great witness and that He should hurry and answer my prayer! I kept praying for *someone* to witness to my dad. Why didn't he meet a Christian who would share the gospel with him?

As I look back, I see that God was preparing me to share with him. I'll never forget the day I was praying for a man to share with my dad, and the Lord whispered in my heart and said, "Will you share with him?" "Not me, Lord, surely there is someone else!" But, what a blessing to see my father come to Christ shortly before he died. God, in His infinite love, wanted me to be there and I had to be who I was at that time in my life to share in the right way.

Because I prayed persistently and was able to see the results, I could not help but be thankful. Over that twenty-three-year period, I learned trust and dependence. God was able to change me in preparation for His way of answering. The process *and* the answer are both worthy of praise.

The blessing of such persevering prayer is unspeakable. There is nothing so heart-searching as the prayer of faith. It teaches you to discover and confess, and give up everything that hinders the coming of the blessing; everything there may be not in accordance with the Father's will. It leads to closer fellowship with Him who alone can teach to pray, to a more entire surrender to draw nigh under no covering but that of the blood, and the Spirit. It calls to a closer and more simple abiding in Christ alone. Christian! Give God time. He will perfect that which concerneth you.[7]

ANDREW MURRAY

Prayer for a Persevering Heart
David was a man after God's heart, and his psalms are full of
praise. Pray with him this prayer of gratitude, and then write
your own prayer of devotion and praise.

DAVID'S PRAYER

But I am like an olive tree
    flourishing in the house of God;
I trust in God's unfailing love for ever and ever.
I will praise you forever for what you have done;
    in your name I will hope, for your name is good.
I will praise you in the presence of your saints.
    (Psalm 52:8-9, NIV)

MY PRAYER

Suggested Scripture Memory
Colossians 4:2

CHAPTER TEN

ACCEPTING GOD'S INVITATION

Hear, O LORD, when I cry with my voice,
And be gracious to me and answer me.
When Thou didst say, "Seek My face,"
my heart said to Thee,
"Thy face, O LORD, I shall seek."
PSALM 27:7-8

One of the first lessons of our Lord in His
school of prayer was: Not to be seen of men.
Enter thy inner chamber; be alone with the
Father. When He has thus taught us that the
meaning of prayer is personal individual
contact with God, He comes with a second
lesson: You have need not only of secret solitary,
but also of public united prayer. And He gives
us a very special promise for the united prayer
of two or three who agree in what they ask.[1]
ANDREW MURRAY

W hat love and tenderness and grace God has bestowed upon us through His invitation to spend time with Him alone in prayer. It amazes me that God ordains prayer for our joy and refreshment and for the privilege of participating in the establishment of His kingdom. He calls us into an intimate relationship through prayer, in which He enables us to know Him and to be transformed into His likeness. This invitation is exclusive to each one of us individually; but it is also inclusive, for God desires to bless us when we, as a body, unite in prayer before His throne.

Prayer of Preparation

As you begin to study, pray with Andrew Murray (twentieth century) for a desire to be intimate with God.

> Lord! teach me to tarry with Thee in the school [of prayer], and give Thee time to train me. May a deep sense of my ignorance, of the wonderful privilege and power of prayer, of the need of the Holy Spirit as the Spirit of prayer, lead me to cast away my thoughts of what I think I know, and make me kneel before Thee in true teachableness and poverty of spirit.[2]

Prayer in Solitude

1. Jesus prayed continually during His ministry. After one of His solitary interludes the disciples asked Him to teach them to pray (Luke 11:1). Read the following passages, and write down the ways in which Jesus is our model in prayer.

Mark 1:35

Luke 5:15-16

2. In the Sermon on the Mount Jesus instructs us regarding secret prayer. Study Matthew 6:5-8 and write down His teaching. Why do you think He emphasizes this particular way to approach God?

> Certainly, if we are to have a quiet hour set down
> in the midst of a hurry of duties, and to keep that time
> inviolate, we must exercise both planning and self-denial.
> We must be prepared to forego many things that are
> pleasant, and some things that are profitable. Let no one
> who can find time for vanities say that they do not have
> enough time for prayer. We have to reclaim our time. It
> may be from recreation, or from social events, or from
> study, or from works of benevolence. Wherever it comes
> from, we must find time every day to enter into our
> closet, and having shut the door, to pray to
> our Father who is in secret.[3]
> DAVID M'INTRYRE

3. Reflect on God's desire for intimacy with you. What is one change you would like to make in order to deepen your relationship with Him through prayer?

4. Spending secret time with the Lord is crucial in responding to His invitation to intimacy, but our relationship isn't put on hold because we leave our closet and go into the world. Read the verses below and record the thoughts and examples concerning prayer in the context of our everyday circumstances.

Nehemiah 2:1-5

1 Thessalonians 5:16-18

> Prayer will be fatiguing to both flesh and blood
> if uttered aloud and sustained long. Oral prayer and
> prayer mentally ordered in words though not spoken
> cannot be engaged in without ceasing. Instead there is an
> undercurrent of prayer that may run continually under
> the stream of our thoughts and never weary us. Such
> prayer is the silent breathing of the Spirit of God
> who dwells in our hearts.[4]
> DAVID M'INTYRE

5. There are times when it is appropriate to accompany prayer with fasting. But God is very specific about why and how we are to fast. What do the following passages teach about this spiritual discipline?

Isaiah 58:1-7

Matthew 6:16-18

> The purpose of fasting is not to get through to God,
> but to allow Him to get through to you. . . . During a fast,
> you should spend the time you would otherwise spend
> eating in prayer and seeking God. . . . You may want to
> start with a short fast. Forgo one meal and use that time
> in prayer and Bible study. . . . Fasting is not a
> requirement. Don't let it become an obligation. God
> should initiate and maintain a fast. It will be a privilege
> and a joy. A time of fasting is a time of real intimacy.[5]
> JENNIFER KENNEDY DEAN

Prayer in Community

6. Praying with others draws us closer to the Lord and to
one another. What promises concerning prayer are given
in Matthew 18:19-20?

> When two or more believers come together to pray,
> they often come with different ideas about what to ask
> and a different understanding about what the will of God
> is in the matter. One may think that God wants to heal
> the sick. Another may think that He is bringing a trial of
> illness to teach the afflicted. But as they seek agreement
> and unity of request, they begin to hear the voice of God
> gradually conforming their differing thoughts . . . into the
> will of God. And their prayer is answered.[6]
> KENT R. WILSON

7. Consider God's promise to two or three gathered together.
How important do you think it is that the group is truly in
agreement, and why?

AUTHOR'S REFLECTION

It is always a delight to receive an invitation from someone
whose company we enjoy. Certainly we have been invited by
God to know Him, to experience Him, and to be a part of His
plan. To refuse such a request seems unthinkable. The eternal,
majestic God of the universe wants to converse with *me*—
how can I say no?

Yet, I find myself declining God's invitation. Why?
Because I am selfish; I am lured away by my own desires. I do
not seek His kingdom first; I do not seek His face. I allow
myself to be distracted. I am too busy.

The Lord says, however, that I do not have to live this
way. I can change. He has extended to me a wonderful call.
He has given me His Spirit to enable me to accept His invita-

tion. I can choose to enter into His secret chamber; I can choose to spend time with friends interceding for what God lays on our hearts and for what will bring Him glory.

I want God's very best. I want to know Him, and I want to see Him act. *The Living Bible* paraphrases Jeremiah 33:3, "Ask me and I will tell you remarkable secrets." How tragic to miss out on any of God's remarkable secrets because I never took enough time to answer His call.

> "Until now you have asked for nothing in My name; ask, and you will receive, that your joy may be made full." (John 16:24)

In His divine condescension God has willed that the working of His Spirit shall follow the prayer of His people. He waits for their intercession, showing the preparation of heart—to what extent they are ready to yield to His Spirit's control.

God rules the world and His Church through the prayers of His people. "That God should have made the extension of His kingdom to such a large extent dependent on the faithfulness of His people in prayer is a stupendous mystery and yet an absolute certainty." God calls for intercessors: in His grace He has made His work dependent on them; He waits for them.[7]
ANDREW MURRAY

Prayer for Seeking God
No one expresses desire quite the way David does. In Psalm 63 he describes his longing for God. May this be your prayer as you seek His face. Add your own expression of longing for God.

DAVID'S PRAYER
O God, Thou art my God; I shall seek Thee earnestly;
My soul thirsts for Thee, my flesh yearns for Thee,
In a dry and weary land where there is no water.
(Psalm 63:1)

Suggested Scripture Memory
Psalm 27:7-8

CHAPTER ELEVEN

SWEET HOUR OF PRAYER

*For a day in Thy courts is better than
a thousand outside.
I would rather stand at the threshold
of the house of my God,
Than dwell in the tents of wickedness.*
PSALM 84:10

*Sweet hour of prayer, sweet hour of prayer,
Thy wings shall my petition bear
To Him whose truth and faithfulness
Engage the waiting soul to bless:
And since He bids me seek His face,
Believe His Word, and trust His grace,
I'll cast on Him my every care,
And wait for thee, sweet hour of prayer.*[1]
WILLIAM W. WALFORD

God's gracious invitation to intimacy through sweet hours of prayer is new every day. We may become disheartened with our prayerlessness, but God continues to ask us to call. Our past failures or vows to be more faithful in prayer should not keep us from responding anew to His desire to communicate His love, His faithfulness, and His desire to be with us. When we respond to His desire for intimacy, prayer becomes a priority and a necessity. We believe with all our heart that a day in His presence is better than a thousand anywhere else.

Prayer of Preparation

As you begin this final session, which will lead you through a time set apart for intimacy with the Lord, pray with Amy Carmichael (twentieth century) for a selfless heart:

> From prayer that asks that I may be
> Sheltered from winds that beat on Thee,
> From fearing when I should aspire,
> From faltering when I should climb higher,
> From silken self, O Captain, free
> Thy soldier who would follow Thee.[2]

> There is no way to learn to pray but by praying. No reasoned philosophy of prayer ever taught a soul to pray. The subject is beset with problems, but there are no problems of prayer to the man who prays . . . and if prayer waits for understanding it will never begin.[3]
> SAMUEL CHADWICK

A Guide to Prayer

The following guide is intended for use either individually or in a group. Before you begin, choose a suitable place and time for spending an intimate interlude with the Lord. If you are meeting as a group, set aside a portion of your time to separate for personal prayer and then gather to share your experiences. In addition to *Becoming a Woman of Prayer* and your Bible, you will find it helpful to bring with you pen and paper (a journal, if you keep one), a hymnbook, and perhaps a favorite devotional book (these additional resources can be especially helpful for extended periods of prayer). The reflection and study you have done in the preceding sessions will provide rich material for you to draw upon during this "sweet hour"—for example, particular Scripture passages that gave you new insights; prayers you wrote that expressed important desires or requests; a quotation that was particularly illuminating. You may adapt this prayer guide for a session of any length, from ten minutes to an hour or even a half-day or more. Use variety as you spend time in prayer: listen, read, pray, sing, walk, sit, kneel, go outside.

ONE: "BE STILL, AND KNOW THAT I AM GOD" (PSALM 46:10, NIV).

Begin by reading a psalm or a verse of Scripture (such as Psalm 46:10, above) to help quiet yourself before God. Enter into the Lord's presence with a period of silence and waiting before Him. Ask Him to prepare and purify your heart.

TWO: "OPEN MY EYES, THAT I MAY BEHOLD WONDERFUL THINGS FROM THY LAW" (PSALM 119:18).

Meditate on a passage of Scripture through which God seems to be speaking to you in a fresh way. If you have a quotation from a devotional writer that helps illuminate that passage, read it alongside the Scripture to aid your meditation.

THREE: "SPEAK, LORD, FOR THY SERVANT IS LISTENING" (1 SAMUEL 3:9).

Now turn your attention from meditation to listening. Ask God to impress upon you what He desires you to learn or experience from meditating on His Word. In preparation for the next step of intercession, ask God to prompt you with the needs He wants you to bring before Him. As you feel free to do so, write down any thoughts or Scriptures prompted by His Spirit.

FOUR: "TRUST IN HIM AT ALL TIMES, O PEOPLE; POUR OUT YOUR HEART BEFORE HIM; GOD IS A REFUGE FOR US" (PSALM 62:8).
Spend time in petition for yourself and intercession for others. You might want to write out your requests, or bring a prayer list with you. Look back over your closing prayers from the previous sessions, as well as prayers of petition and intercession in the Bible, to guide you in pouring out your heart before the Lord.

FIVE: "FOR GOD IS THE KING OF ALL THE EARTH; SING PRAISES WITH A SKILLFUL PSALM" (PSALM 47:7).
Spend time praising and thanking God—aloud or silently, singing or playing an instrument, or writing out your praise. Use a hymnbook, the Psalms, or other Scripture passages that will lead you in glorifying God.

SIX: "MY SOUL WAITS IN SILENCE FOR GOD ONLY; FROM HIM IS MY SALVATION" (PSALM 62:1).
Close your interlude of intimacy in silent reflection and communion. Ask the Lord to keep your heart sensitive to His Spirit as you leave this time of prayer.

> You can do more than pray, after you have prayed. But you can *not* do more than pray *until* you have prayed.[4]
> S. D. GORDON

AUTHOR'S REFLECTION
"Sweet hour of prayer," sings the hymnwriter. Communion with our Lord is indeed sweet—a precious privilege that brings joy to our souls. This study is just one of many helpful books and guides on prayer available to us today—but our motive in studying prayer should not be to master guides or lists, but to behold our God, to dwell in His pres-

ence, to become an instrument used for His glory.

Prayer is a gracious invitation from our heavenly Father for intimacy and partnership in accomplishing His purposes. That He answers, and that He blesses us abundantly more than we could ask or think, demonstrates His loving desire for us to know Him and trust Him for our good.

The world offers temporary and fleeting refreshment; God invites us to an eternally enriching relationship through sweet hours of prayer . . . sweet not only to us, but to our Lord. Truly, a day in His courts is better than a thousand outside.

All the world knows now of old Père Chaffangeon, who used to remain for hours before the altar in the church at Ars without even moving his lips; it seems that he was speaking to God.

"And what do you say to Him?" the Curé asked.

"Oh," replied the old peasant, "He looks at me, and I look at Him."

"The greatest of mystics," says Henri Ghéon, "have found no formula more simple, more exact, more complete, more sublime, to express the conversation of the soul with God."[5]
WILLIAM E. SANGSTER

A Prayer for Sweet Hours with the Lord

David's one request was to be in the presence of God. Pray with David for a heart attuned to consistent communion with God. Consider adding your own prayer for dwelling with the Lord in sweet hours and moments of intimacy with Him.

DAVID'S PRAYER

One thing I have asked from the LORD, that I shall seek:
That I may dwell in the house of the LORD all the days
    of my life,
To behold the beauty of the LORD,
And to meditate in His temple,

For in the day of trouble He will conceal me in His
    tabernacle;
In the secret place of His tent He will hide me;
He will lift me up on a rock.
(Psalm 27:4-5)

Suggested Scripture Memory
Psalm 84:10

NOTES

Chapter One—An Invitation to Intimacy

1. Martin Smith, "God Is a Conversation," *Union Life Magazine*, vol. 18, no. 4 (May/June 1993), p. 8.
2. Julian of Norwich, quoted in *Prayers Across the Centuries* (Wheaton, Ill.: Harold Shaw, 1993), p. 80.
3. O. Hallesby, *Prayer* (London: Inter-Varsity, 1959), p. 7.
4. Charles Spurgeon, *The Power of Prayer in a Believer's Life*, Robert Hall, ed. (Lynnwood, Wash.: Emerald Books, 1993), p. 22.
5. John Owen, in *The Treasury of David*, Charles Spurgeon, ed. (McLean, Va.: MacDonald, n.d.), p. 313.
6. Oswald Chambers, *My Utmost for His Highest* (Westwood, N.J.: Barbour & Co., 1935), 28 August.

Chapter Two—Praying in Faith

1. O. Hallesby, *Prayer* (London: Inter-Varsity, 1959), p. 25.
2. John D. Grassmic on Mark 11:22-24, *The Bible Knowledge Commentary: New Testament Edition*, John F. Walvoord and Roy B. Zuck, ed. (Wheaton, Ill.: Victor, 1983), p. 158.
3. Thomas à Kempis, quoted in *Prayers Across the Centuries* (Wheaton, Ill.: Harold Shaw, 1993), p. 81.
4. S. D. Gordon, *Quiet Talks on Prayer* (New York: Grosset & Dunlap/Revell, 1941), p. 150.
5. Grassmic, pp. 158-59.
6. R. A. Torrey, *How to Pray* (Chicago: Moody, 1960), pp. 50-51.
7. Ray Palmer, "My Faith Looks Up to Thee" (1808–1887).
8. Charles Spurgeon, *The Power of Prayer in a Believer's Life*, Robert Hall, ed. (Lynnwood, Wash.: Emerald Books, 1993), p. 35.

Chapter Three—God's Help in Prayer

1. Lloyd John Ogilvie, *You Can Pray with Power* (Ventura, Calif.: Regal, 1988), p. 28.
2. S. D. Gordon, *Quiet Talks on Prayer* (New York: Grosset & Dunlap/Revell, 1941), p. 187.
3. E. M. Bounds, *The Complete Works of E. M. Bounds on Prayer: Book Four, The Reality of Prayer* (Grand Rapids, Mich.: Baker, 1990), p. 286.
4. Oswald Chambers, *My Utmost for His Highest* (Westwood, N.J.: Barbour & Co., 1935), 8 November.
5. R. A. Torrey, *How to Pray* (Chicago: Moody, 1960), p. 57.
6. Charles Spurgeon, *The Power of Prayer in a Believer's Life*, Robert Hall, ed. (Lynnwood, Wash.: Emerald Books, 1993), pp. 39, 41.
7. Torrey, pp. 47, 61.

Chapter Four—Delighting in God

1. Charles Spurgeon, *The Treasury of David*, vol. 1, part 2 (McLean, Va.: MacDonald, n.d.), p. 171.
2. Amy Carmichael, quoted in Stuart and Brenda Blanch, *Learning of God: Readings from Amy Carmichael* (Fort Washington, Penn.: Christian Literature Crusade, 1985), p. 59.
3. Jennifer Kennedy Dean, *Heart's Cry* (Birmingham, Ala.: New Hope, 1992), p. 2.
4. Andrew Murray, *Prayer: A 31-Day Plan to Enrich Your Prayer Life* (Uhrichsville, Ohio: Barbour & Co., n.d.), p. 40.
5. Charles Spurgeon, *The Power of Prayer in a Believer's Life*, Robert Hall, ed. (Lynnwood, Wash.: Emerald Books, 1993), pp. 109-10.
6. Matthew Henry, *Commentary on the Whole Bible* (Iowa Falls, Iowa: Riverside, n.d.), vol. 3, p. 370.

Chapter Five—God's Answers

1. Mary B. M. Duncan, in *The Treasury of David*, vol. 2 (McLean, Va.: MacDonald, n.d.), p. 112.
2. Saint Ignatius of Loyola, in *Prayers Across the Centuries* (Wheaton, Ill.: Harold Shaw, 1993), p. 89.
3. Oswald Chambers, *My Utmost for His Highest* (Westwood, N.J.: Barbour & Co., 1935), 7 February.
4. O. Hallesby, *Prayer* (London: Inter-Varsity, 1959), pp. 39-40.

5. D. Martyn Lloyd-Jones, *Faith Tried and Triumphant* (Grand Rapids, Mich.: Baker, 1953), pp. 10-11.
6. Frederick W. Robertson, in *Classic Sermons on Prayer*, compiled by Warren W. Wiersbe (Grand Rapids, Mich.: Kregel, 1987), pp. 47-49.
7. Richard C. Halverson, *Perspective* (Washington, D.C.: Concern, Inc.), vol. 25, no. 45, 7 November 1973.
8. S. D. Gordon, *Quiet Talks on Prayer* (New York: Grosset & Dunlap/Revell, 1941), pp. 53-54.

Chapter Six—When God Is Silent

1. Philip Yancey, *Disappointment with God* (Grand Rapids, Mich.: Zondervan, 1988), p. 207.
2. Benjamin Jenks, in *Prayers Across the Centuries* (Wheaton, Ill.: Harold Shaw, 1993), p. 99.
3. R. A. Torrey, *How to Pray* (Chicago: Moody, 1960), p. 69.
4. Oswald Chambers, *The Oswald Chambers Daily Devotional Bible* (Nashville, Tenn.: Thomas Nelson, 1992), p. 507.
5. Lloyd John Ogilvie, *You Can Pray with Power* (Ventura, Calif.: Regal, 1988), p. 92.
6. David M'Intyre, *The Hidden Life of Prayer* (Minneapolis, Minn.: Bethany, 1993), p. 51.

Chapter Seven—The Lord's Pattern of Prayer

1. C. Samuel Storms, *Reaching God's Ear* (Wheaton, Ill.: Tyndale, 1988), p. 23.
2. John Wesley, in *Prayers Across the Centuries* (Wheaton, Ill.: Harold Shaw, 1993), p. 110.
3. C. S. Lewis, *Letters to Malcom: Chiefly on Prayer* (New York: Harcourt Brace Jovanovich, 1964), p. 28.
4. Paul Thigpen, "Lead Us Not into Temptation," *Discipleship Journal* (March/April 1991), vol. 11, no. 2, pp. 41-42.
5. J. Oswald Sanders, *Prayer Power Unlimited* (Minneapolis, Minn.: World Wide Publications, 1977), p. 94.

Chapter Eight—Intercessory Prayer

1. Oswald Chambers, *My Utmost for His Highest* (Westwood, N.J.: Barbour & Co., 1935), 4 May.
2. Saint Polycarp, in *Prayers Across the Centuries* (Wheaton, Ill.: Harold Shaw, 1993), p. 50.

3. S. D. Gordon, *Quiet Talks on Prayer* (New York: Grosset & Dunlap/Revell, 1941), pp. 111-12.
4. C. Samuel Storms, *Reaching God's Ear* (Wheaton, Ill.: Tyndale, 1988), p. 193.
5. Eugene Peterson, *Where Your Treasure Is* (Grand Rapids, Mich.: Eerdmans, 1985), p. 6.
6. Lloyd John Ogilvie, *You Can Pray with Power* (Ventura, Calif.: Regal, 1988), p. 78.
7. Amy Carmichael, quoted in Stuart and Brenda Blanch, *Learning of God: Readings from Amy Carmichael* (Fort Washington, Penn.: Christian Literature Crusade, 1985), p. 59.

Chapter Nine—Persevering in Prayer

1. R. A. Torrey, *How to Pray* (Chicago: Moody, 1960), p. 48.
2. George Herbert, in *Prayers Across the Centuries* (Wheaton, Ill.: Harold Shaw, 1993), p. 98.
3. J. Oswald Sanders, *Prayer Power Unlimited* (Minneapolis, Minn.: World Wide Publications, 1977), pp. 71-72.
4. Torrey, pp. 54-55.
5. Matthew Henry, *Commentary on the Whole Bible* (Iowa Falls, Iowa: Riverside, n.d.), vol. 2, p. 248.
6. Jennifer Kennedy Dean, *Heart's Cry* (Birmingham, Ala.: New Hope, 1992), p. 48.
7. Andrew Murray, *With Christ in the School of Prayer* (Old Tappan, N.J.: Revell, 1953), p. 90.

Chapter Ten—Accepting God's Invitation

1. Andrew Murray, *With Christ in the School of Prayer* (Old Tappan, N.J.: Revell, 1953), p. 82.
2. Murray, p. 17.
3. David M'Intyre, *The Hidden Life of Prayer* (Minneapolis, Minn.: Bethany, 1993), p. 39.
4. M'Intyre, p. 30.
5. Jennifer Kennedy Dean, *Heart's Cry* (Birmingham, Ala.: New Hope, 1992), p. 105.
6. Kent R. Wilson, "The Lost Art of Group Prayer," *Discipleship Journal* (March/April 1994), issue 80, p. 44.
7. Andrew Murray, *Prayer: A 31-Day Plan to Enrich Your Prayer Life* (Uhrichsville, Ohio: Barbour & Co., n.d.), p. 10.

Chapter Eleven—Sweet Hour of Prayer
1. William W. Walford, "Sweet Hour of Prayer," *Hymns for the Family of God* (Nashville, Tenn.: Paragon Associates, 1976), no. 439.
2. Amy Carmichael, quoted in *A Chance to Die: The Life and Legacy of Amy Carmichael*, by Elisabeth Elliot (Old Tappan, N.J.: Revell, 1987), p. 221.
3. Samuel Chadwick, quoted in *Praying from God's Heart*, by Lee Brase with Henry Helsabeck (Colorado Springs: NavPress, 1993), p. 12.
4. S. D. Gordon, *Quiet Talks on Prayer* (New York: Grosset & Dunlap/Revell, 1941), p. 16.
5. William E. Sangster, in *Classic Sermons on Prayer*, compiled by Warren W. Wiersbe (Grand Rapids, Mich.: Kregel, 1987), p. 157.

AUTHOR

Cynthia Hall Heald is a native Texan. She and her husband, Jack, a veterinarian by profession, are on full-time staff with The Navigators in Tucson, Arizona. They have four children: Melinda, Daryl, Shelly, and Michael.

Cynthia graduated from the University of Texas with a B.A. in English. She speaks frequently to church women's groups and at seminars and retreats.

Cynthia is also the author of the NavPress Bible studies *Becoming a Woman of Excellence; Becoming a Woman of Freedom; Becoming a Woman of Purpose; Intimacy with God: Pursuing a Deeper Experience of God Through the Psalms;* and *Loving Your Husband: Building an Intimate Marriage in a Fallen World* (companion study to *Loving Your Wife: Building an Intimate Marriage in a Fallen World* by Jack and Cynthia Heald).

SMALL-GROUP MATERIALS FROM NAVPRESS

BIBLE STUDY SERIES

DESIGN FOR DISCIPLESHIP
GOD IN YOU
GOD'S DESIGN FOR THE FAMILY
INSTITUTE OF BIBLICAL
  COUNSELING Series
LEARNING TO LOVE Series

LIFECHANGE
RADICAL RELATIONSHIPS
SPIRITUAL DISCIPLINES
STUDIES IN CHRISTIAN LIVING
THINKING THROUGH DISCIPLESHIP

TOPICAL BIBLE STUDIES

Becoming a Woman of Excellence
Becoming a Woman of Freedom
Becoming a Woman of Prayer
Becoming a Woman of Purpose
The Blessing Study Guide
Homemaking
Intimacy with God
Loving Your Husband

Loving Your Wife
A Mother's Legacy
Praying From God's Heart
Surviving Life in the Fast Lane
To Run and Not Grow Tired
To Walk and Not Grow Weary
What God Does When Men Pray
When the Squeeze Is On

BIBLE STUDIES WITH COMPANION BOOKS

Bold Love
Daughters of Eve
The Discipline of Grace
The Feminine Journey
Inside Out
The Masculine Journey
The Practice of Godliness
The Pursuit of Holiness

Secret Longings of the Heart
Spiritual Disciplines
Tame Your Fears
Transforming Grace
Trusting God
What Makes a Man?
The Wounded Heart

RESOURCES

Brothers!
Discipleship Journal's 101 Best
  Small-Group Ideas
How to Build a Small-Groups Ministry
How to Lead Small Groups
Jesus Cares for Women
The Navigator Bible Studies
  Handbook

The Small Group Leaders
  Training Course
Topical Memory System
  (KJV/NIV and NASB/NKJV)
Topical Memory System:
  Life Issues